JERSEY

Through the Lens Again

St Helier Harbour.

JERSEY
Through the Lens Again

Compiled by

**Elizabeth Bois,
H. M. de Ste. Croix
and Alan Young**
of the Société Jersiaise

Phillimore

1989

Published by
PHILLIMORE & CO. LTD.,
Shopwyke Hall, Chichester, Sussex

ISBN 0 85033 719 4

Printed and bound in Great Britain by
BIDDLES LTD.,
Guildford, Surrey

List of Illustrations

Frontispiece: St Helier Harbour

St Helier Street Scenes
1. Beresford Street, *c*.1920
2. No. 6 Caledonia Place
3. Church Street
4. Clare Villas, Clare Street
5. Commercial Buildings
6. David Place, looking north
7. St Aubin's Road, at First Tower
8. Demolition of the Green Street engine sheds, 1967
9. Demolition of the Old Government House, 1962
10. Demolition of Grosvenor House, 1962
11. Halkett Place
12. & 13. Dumaresq Street
14. New Street including the Cercle St Thomas
15. No. 53 Paradise Row, New Street
16. The old H.M.V. sign on the gable of Mr. Foot's gramophone shop
17. The Royal Square, looking east
18. Another view of the Royal Square, *c*.1890
19. The Royal Square, looking west
20. The interior of the Royal Court in 1906
21. The 3rd Battalion of the Royal Jersey Militia, 1914

Shops and Services
22. J. Pallot, hatter, hosier and shirtmaker
23. Noel and Porter in King Street
24. Brooks' and A. de Gruchy and Co. in King Street
25. The junction between King Street and New Street, *c*.1915
26. Queen Street, *c*.1907
27. T. H. Le Cornu's shop in the angle of Minden Street, 1928
28. C. G. Ferbrache's antiques shop, Snow Hill
29. Vine Street, north of Royal Square
30. Le Riche's Stores with staff
31. Le Riche's Stores
32. Woods Bros., chemists, at No. 4 Beresford Street, 1880
33. A. Quenouillere
34. A fire-fighting group, *c*.1886
35. The Central Manual Telephone Exchange in 1926
36. The bottling plant at F. G. de Faye's, 1917

37. Bicycle shop display, pre-1914
38. A firm supplying boilers and lawn mowers, *c*.1900
39. A. H. and W. C. Bryant's Rock and Brick Company's brickfields
40. Le Rondin Laundry in St John, *c*.1899

Harbours and Shipping
41. The new North Quay under construction
42. The Inner Harbour
43. Pier Road and harbours
44. La Folie and French Harbour
45. St Helier Harbour from West Mount
46. The Weighbridge, showing the lifeboat house
47. The Weighbridge in 1907
48. St Aubin's Harbour with the Bulwarks and the *Somerville Hotel*
49. The esplanade at St Aubin's
50. St Brelade's Bay
51. St Catherine's Bay: a harbour of refuge
52. The S.S. *Mistletoe* in Gorey Harbour
53. Anne Port: an early 20th-century view
54. Rozel Bay from Le Saie
55. Bouley Bay
56. Shipbuilding yards at Gorey, *c*.1860
57. The Albert Pier in St Helier Harbour
58. Cargo boats in St Helier Harbour
59. St Helier Harbour from South Hill
60. The Upper Harbour and Fort Regent
61. The S.S. *Caesarea* caught aground on 7 July 1923
62. The S.S. *Roebuck* lying at the New North Quay
63. The S.S. *Roebuck*
64. The S.S. *Stella* leaving harbour
65. The Casquets lighthouse off the west coast of Alderney

Railways and Aviation
66. A Western Railway train, St Aubin's station, 1906
67. A train at Fauvic on the Eastern line
68. The Eastern Railway terminus at Gorey
69. The Eastern Railway railcar, the *Brittany*, *c*.1928
70. First Tower station on the Western line

71. Don Bridge station in St Brelade
72. The interior of the old St Aubin's terminus
73. St Aubin's terminus, now St Brelade's Parish Hall
74. La Haule station house in 1936
75. The original West Park Pavilion
76. Lunch party for the opening of Jersey Railways in 1870
77. Jurat de Quetteville raising the Clameur de Haro, c.1869
78. A DH Dragon on the beach
79. The *Cloud of Iona*, a SARO A 19
80. A SARO Windhover
81. A Supermarine Seagull Flying Boat, in St Helier Harbour
82. DH 86 Express and DH Dragons on the beach, 1934
83. A DH 84 coming in to land at West Park
84. A closer view showing Elizabeth Castle
85. *Ouaisné Bay* at the opening of the Airport in 1937

Agriculture
86. Cows being tethered after haymaking
87. 'Le Rué Golden Princess'
88. Another aristocrat, 'Beauchamp Sybil Reviver'
89. Cows tethered to conserve pasture
90. A Gascoigne Bail milking machine
91. An apple-crusher, dated 1772, converted for horticulture
92. An apple-crusher in operation
93. John Dorey, a cider merchant, at Brook Farm, St John
94. Potato planting at Bouley Bay
95. Potato clamps in St Lawrence, summer 1940
96. Going over the 'bridge, weighing empty and full barrels
97. Lorry-loads of 'earlies' at the Weighbridge about 1950
98. Conway Street at the height of the potato season
99. Tomato picking at L'Etacq
100. The States Experimental Farm, Trinity
101. The most usual basic Jersey cart
102. Versatile four-wheeled van
103. The great plough being used in double harness
104. An alternative ploughing technique
105. Vraicing at Le Hocq

Island Life and Events
106. Ceremony at Victoria College
107. The Victoria College Cricket XI in 1867
108. A loan exhibition in Victoria College, 1916
109. An excursion to the Devil's Hole in 1903
110. Members of a coach outing at Grève de Lecq

111. St Aubin's Bay in the days of the bathing machine
112. Troops of the Royal Artillery at Elizabeth Castle
113. Messrs. P. Mallet, P. Luce, J. Le Maistre and C. F. Le Feuvre, of the Royal Militia
114. General Gough with the Ladies' Rifle Club, c.1907
115. Prisoners of War Camp under construction, 1915
116. Military exercises at Les Platons: 4.7 guns
117. The Jubilee Dinner at Victoria College in 1902
118. A Government House garden party, c.1909
119. Another view of guests on the lawn
120. Guests leaving Government House
121. St Helier's parish church bazaar and fête, 1908
122. Laying the foundation stone for the *Grand Hotel*, 1890
123. King George V and Queen Mary's Silver Jubilee in 1935
124. King Street decorated for the Silver Jubilee
125. Queen Street vies with King Street on the same occasion
126. Battle of Jersey centenary celebrations in Royal Square
127. Island choirs on the People's Park, Westmount, 1902
128. The Vicomte reads the Declaration of War, 4 August 1914
129. The Battle of Flowers in 1912
130. The Battle of Flowers at Springfield Football Ground
131. An early Battle of Flowers on Victoria Avenue
132. The Concours Musical, c.1912
133. Drill practice on the Parade Ground at Fort Regent
134. Jersey Ladies' College
135. Headmistress's entrance at the College

Personalities
136. Major N. V. L. Rybot in the Suez Canal area in 1914
137. Mr. A. C. Godfray, in his masonic regalia
138. A Buchan-Ireland wedding party at Le Bocage, 1872
139. The Very Rev. G. O. Balleine, M.A., Dean of Jersey
140. Mr. J. Sinel, naturalist and archaeologist
141. Mr. E. T. Nicolle
142. Miss Emmeline Augusta Barreau
143. Mr. E. T. Touzel, lifeboatman
144. Judge 'Johnny' Pinel
145. Mr. Ralph Mollet
146. Jack Counter, V.C.

147. Père Burdo and Professor C. B. McBurney, archaeologists
148. Unveiling a plaque commemorating the fallen French residents of Jersey in World War One

General Views
149. St Catherine's Bay
150. La Collette: the Ladies' Bathing Place, *c.*1910
151. La Collette: the Jersey Swimming Club's diving stage
152. Grève de Lecq
153. Grève de Lecq, showing a camera obscura
154. Plemont: toll-bearing staircases
155. The entrance to Valley des Vaux
156. L'Etacq, with *Queens Hotel* and the *Star Hotel*

157. An archer's-eye view of Gorey Harbour and Grouville Bay
158. La Corbière lighthouse
159. A close-up view of the lighthouse
160. Hamptonne, St Lawrence
161. Hamptonne
162. Seymour Tower
163. Seafield House, Millbrook
164. St Helier from the west, *c.*1879
165. The *British Hotel* in Broad Street
166. The *Hotel Imperial*, St Saviour's Road
167. Mont Mado
168. Platte Rocque
169. Gorey Hill in 1896
170. Statue of Queen Victoria at Weighbridge
171. St Helier Harbour with deep-sea fishing boats
172. High Tower, St Ouen, *c.*1935

Acknowledgements

The compilers wish to record their thanks to the following for their donations to the Société Jersiaise of photographs which have been chosen for this book:

Jean Arthur	90
Brig. H. G. L. Brain	21
Robin Briault	33, 34, 56, 67, 85, 93, 97, 99, 160, 161
E. Dale	66
R. de Faye	36
M. Ginns	172
Jersey Evening Post	8, 9, 10, 65, 79, 95, 100, 123, 124, 125
T. H. Le Cornu	27
R. H. Mayne	12, 13, 144
R. Miles	163
L. Le Moignan	102
H. de C. Mourant	22
Maj. T. E. Naish, R.E.	115
Mr. Oldridge	80
M. H. Peck	2
A. Renouf	61
M. J. H. Richardson	89, 133
Albert Smith	5, 7, 14, 24, 29, 30, 37, 39, 48, 50, 52, 54, 64, 86, 87, 98, 109, 110, 111, 121, 131, 153, 158, 159, 162, 165, 170
Joan Stevens	40, 51, 77, 91, 138
M. Sutton	68
Mrs. Toy	92
Mr. Voisin	62

Introduction

In preparing this second book of *Jersey through the Lens* we have made full use of the increasing amount of material provided by donations to the Société Jersiaise during the 14 years since the first volume was published.

The categories presented by the compilers of the original work have been largely retained. Several have been covered more widely, depending on the number of photographs now available, others less so. Some extra sections have been added, because they seemed to provide fresh pictorial interest. For instance, there are more photographs of the town of St Helier in olden days; and there is a wider selection of general views. It was the aim of the first book to present Jersey as it was about a century ago. This edition will naturally bring the story more up to date.

The same aspects of life in the island are basically visible today, despite the vast changes which have been and are still taking place. Thus this book displays the 'Jersey That Was', always of interest to both residents and tourists. It is hoped that it will bring a similar pleasure to those who are developing, or still retain, an affection for Jersey. This was certainly the hope of Joan Stevens and Richard Mayne, to whose memory we all owe a great debt for compiling the first volume.

Rather than write introductions to each section, which would tend to be too repetitive, we summarise the main sections here. It is thought that the captions to each photograph will lead readers to seek further historical information for themselves. Much opportunity for such study exists in the Société Jersiaise Library in the Museum.

If Jersey is to retain its true character it must preserve its rural element. Though some important customs connected with agriculture still survive, the general scene has much altered. Tomatoes are now largely grown under glass. Cauliflowers and calabrese are frequent crops and potatoes are to be seen on all sides, though the fields are often sadly disfigured in spring by plastic covering. Vraic is still highly esteemed as a fertiliser. Jersey cattle are, of course, of international importance and active steps are continually being taken to improve the breed.

For more than 600 years, until 1946, the compulsory Militia played an important part in the lives of the men of Jersey, not least in its readiness to defend the island. This subject was well covered in the first book, so it has only been touched upon here.

Ships were being built in Jersey for the cod fisheries in the 18th century, but it was not until about 1820 that permanent shipyards were established. By 1860 there were 18 shipyards along the south coast and at Gorey. But the industry collapsed dramatically with the advent of iron and steam. St Aubin, so well protected from the prevailing south-westerly winds, was the main harbour until the mid-19th century, when the Victoria and Albert piers were constructed in St Helier. Much benefit accrued to passenger traffic when the rail link from Southampton to London was opened in 1840. Over the years there followed a succession of mail steamers, valuable indeed, though the crossing was uncomfortable in winter.

The first island railway was established in 1870. The inaugural train did the run from St Helier to St Aubin in 9½ minutes. On that great day there was a celebratory luncheon at Noirmont Manor for 180 people. The extension of the Jersey Western to the Corbière through beautiful countryside was completed in 1899. In 1873 a start was made on a line to run eventually from St Helier right along the coast to Gorey harbour.

In the town of St Helier, the Royal Square is revealed as the focal point of important occasions. Elsewhere, despite much demolition, it is good to find that some fine old frontages have survived and the Market has altered little since it was opened in 1887. Shops, however, have changed greatly. There are now far fewer smaller ones, with the owner living above his shop. People were more closely linked to each other in those days. Untroubled by motor traffic, the streets were pleasanter, and safer, places; clothes were simpler and more uniform and the atmosphere more homely. Much trouble must have been taken to decorate the streets and provide fun and entertainment for notable occasions. In the portrait section it has been our aim not only to reproduce some excellent photographs, but also to draw attention to the services rendered in the past for the benefit of the Société and the island.

Finally we hope that the general views emphasise what a splendid setting Jersey provides for the manifold activities of life to which this collection bears witness.

The compilers of this volume are most grateful to the staff of the Société Jersiaise and Jersey Museums Service especially Mr. George Drew and Mrs. Marion Bickerton for their help, and to Mr. G. J. C. Bois for preparing a duplicate record of all the original photographs for retention in the Société's Archives room. The Archives of the Société Jersiaise almost certainly contain sufficient material to make a further selection of photographs for publication possible in due course.

St Helier Street Scenes

1. Beresford Street, *c*.1920. This street, which dates from the 1820s, is on the north side of the Market. It is named after Lord Beresford, a Peninsular War General and Marshal of the Portuguese Army, who became the last Governor of Jersey.

2. No. 6 Caledonia Place. The gable is part of La Longue Caserne, believed to have been originally built as a cod drying shed, and later occupied as a Barracks. It is shortly to be incorporated into the new Museum complex.

3. Church Street. The Wine Vaults is now The United Club. W. Laffoley's premises is now The States Building. The street's old name is 'La Rue de Trousse Cotillon' or 'Lash your Petticoats Down Street', owing to the bitter easterly winds which can sweep across from the Royal Square, as well as the prevailing south-westerly wind coming up from the sea.

4. Clare Villas, Clare Street.

5. Commercial Buildings, part of a long stretch facing the Harbour.

6. David Place, looking north towards St Mark's church. Notice the milk cart, a type in use until 1945.

7. St Aubin's Road, at First Tower.

8. Demolition of the Green Street engine and carriage sheds, 1967. These sheds were erected soon after the station which was opened in August 1873. The site was used as a bus garage from the closure of the railway in June 1929 until it became part of the new Route du Fort.

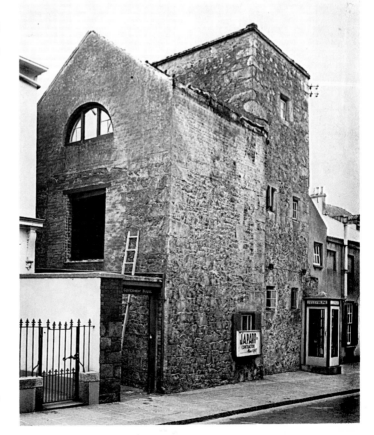

9. Demolition in 1962 of the Old Government House, at the corner of La Motte Street and Grosvenor Street, now a garage. Here, the French troops in 1781 surprised Governor Corbet in his nightgown.

10. Demolition of Grosvenor House, now the Commercial Union Building, 1962.

11. Halkett Place, with the entrance to French Lane on the right. This street is named after Sir Colin Halkett, the first Lt.-Governor to reside in the present Government House in St Saviour, in the 1820s.

12. & 13. Dumaresq Street, and the corner of Hue Street, where buildings dated from the 18th century, and parts might have been earlier. It had until very recently been hoped to save them for museum purposes as a socio-industrial commercial complex embracing a forge, a carpenter's shop and a bakery, but an architectural survey revealed that the structures had become dangerous and the rescue attempt had to be abandoned.

14. New Street. On the left is the Cercle St Thomas, 1842, and in the background the new St Thomas's church of 1885.

15. No. 53 Paradise Row, New Street, showing C. P. and W. W. Ouless, R.A. outside the home and studio of P. J. Ouless, the marine painter, 1817-85.

16. The old H.M.V. sign painted by George Dean in 1917 on the gable of Mr. Foot's shop, a tribute to the materials which have withstood over 70 years of channel gales and sometimes tropical summers. Mr. Foot was originally a gramophone and record dealer.

17. The Royal Square, looking east, before the building of the States House of Assembly.

18.   Another view of the Royal Square, *c*.1890, showing the States House of Assembly, but before the Public Library was added at the west end of the Royal Court.

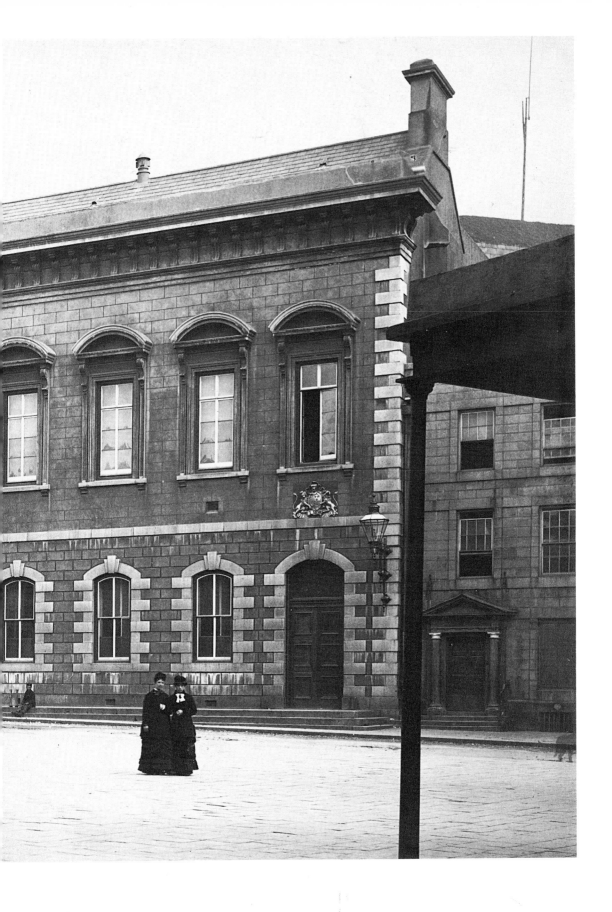

19. The Royal Square, looking west, showing the United Club which dates from 1825.

20. The interior of the Royal Court in 1906.

21. The 3rd Battalion of the Royal Jersey Militia marching from the New Cut into King Street on their return from the Don Bridge camp on 15 July 1914. They are led by their C.O., Col. G. M. Mackenzie.

Shops and Services

22. J. Pallot, hatter, hosier and shirtmaker, at 31 King Street. This family business flourished from the late 1800s to 1908.

23. Noel and Porter in King Street, now British Home Stores.

24. Brooks' and A. de Gruchy and Co. in King Street. Brooks' was an established family newsagent's business for over two generations, father and various sons being involved in several branches. Like many other small family concerns locally, the business was ultimately sold. Abraham de Gruchy, member of a Huguenot family, opened a small drapery shop in 1810 in St Peter. He moved to these premises in St Helier in 1826 and a limited liability company was formed in 1886. The business has developed over the years into a large general departmental store, incorporating two restaurants.

25.   The junction between King Street and New Street, *c*.1915.

26.   Queen Street, *c*.1907, looking west with Boot's shop on the right.

27.   T. H. Le Cornu's shop in the angle of Minden Street, 1928. Blue Stone was the familiar term for copper sulphate crystals, then used in solution as a spray for tomatoes.

28. C. G. Ferbrache's antiques shop at the foot of the ramp at Snow Hill. The site is now that of the Midland Bank Trust Corporation (Jersey) Ltd.

29.   Vine Street, north of the Royal Square. The *York Hotel* is now Collins Ltd.

30. Le Riche's Stores with staff, at the corner of Beresford Street and Halkett Place. This business was founded in 1897 and is now the biggest store in the Islands for groceries, wines and spirits as well as household goods of every description.

31. An earlier picture of Le Riche's Stores.

32. Woods Bros., chemists, at No. 4 Beresford Street. The lane on the left is Cattle Street. This photograph was taken in 1880.

33. A. Quenouillere, on the corner of Pitt Street and King Street. Since being a bicycle shop, it has been occupied by several businesses including a printer's, a dance hall and restaurant. The business is now Senett and Spears' photographic and perfumery store. The original Victorian frontage has been repeatedly modernised.

34. A fire-fighting group, *c*.1886, when the Paid Police were also the Town Fire Brigade.

35. The Central Manual Telephone Exchange in 1926.

36. The bottling plant at F. G. de Faye's, the chemists, in 1917. They had an artesian well and purveyed still and aerated water. Note the syphons in the foreground.

37.   Professor Willmore, bronze medallist, at an Exhibition of uncertain date but probably before 1914. Note the advertisement for a bicycle riding school. The concept of single tube tyres, repairable from the outside in two minutes, must have made considerable impact.

38.   An unknown firm supplying boilers, chaff-cutters, lawn mowers, pulpers and bicycles, probably *c.* 1900.

39. A. H. and W. C. Bryant's Rock and Brick Company's brickfields in Bellozanne Valley in 1884. It was sold as a going concern in 1887 to outside buyers who dispersed it among various purchasers; perhaps an early exercise in asset stripping.

40. Le Rondin Laundry in St John, *c.*1899, run by the Morel family. The Morels, originally a farming family to judge from their premises, took in the laundry of the Jesuit College in St Saviour. As the numbers at the College ran into hundreds this must, in the days of handwashing, have been a full-time operation. The Jesuit fathers were recalled to France about the time of World War Two, but the Morel Laundry has long since vanished from the scene with the advent of more modern facilities.

Harbours and Shipping

41.   The New North Quay under construction.

42.   The Inner Harbour with the beginning of the New North Quay just visible in the right centre and, on the left, a glimpse of what later became the Victoria Gardens. Note the horse-drawn roller awaiting use on the right.

43. Pier Road pre-tarmac, and harbours. The
small military quarters in the upper right centre
later became the Motor Traffic Office.

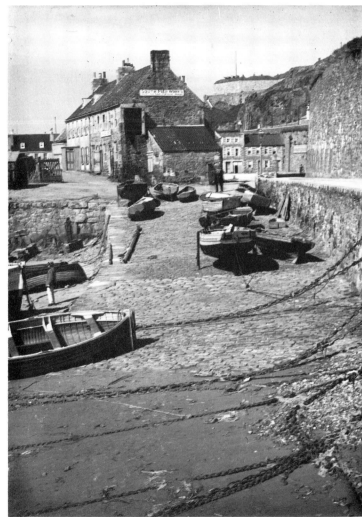

44. The Old Harbour and South Pier Iron
Works, later La Folie. Note the guns on Fort
Regent in the background.

45. St Helier Harbour from West Mount. The roof of the bandstand in Triangle Park is just visible in the right centre.

46. The Weighbridge, showing the lifeboat house, railway refreshment rooms and train shed. Also note the Westaway monument, later moved to the foot of the hill leading down to Victoria Quay.

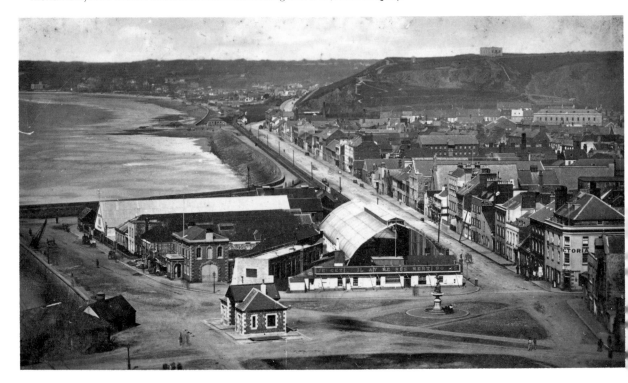

47. At the Weighbridge in 1907. The *Pomme d'Or Hotel* bus is waiting to meet the boats, with its upper deck ready for luggage.

48. St Aubin's Harbour with the Bulwarks and the *Somerville Hotel* in the background. This prominent building was opened in 1880.

49. The esplanade at St Aubin's, showing the quay and the old railway terminus.

50. St Brelade's Bay.

51. St Catherine's Bay: a harbour of refuge. The distant breakwater was built between 1847 and 1852, when there was concern about the new French forts on the other side of the water.

52.   The S.S. *Mistletoe* in Gorey Harbour.

53.   Anne Port: an early 20th-century view. Note the gun on top of Victoria Tower on the skyline and the cider apple trees in the foreground.

54.   Rozel Bay from Le Saie.

55. Bouley Bay. Note the absence of trees, and the hotel, now much enlarged.

56. Shipbuilding yards at Gorey, *c*.1860.

57.   The Albert Pier in St Helier Harbour with Elizabeth Castle in the background.

58.   Cargo boats in St Helier Harbour.

59.   St Helier Harbour from South Hill.

60. The Upper Harbour from the west with Fort Regent on the skyline.

61. The S.S. *Caesarea* caught aground in the shallow waters between the pier and Elizabeth Castle on 7 July 1923.

62. The second S.S. *Roebuck* lying at the New North Quay. This vessel ran on the Weymouth-Channel Islands cargo service.

63. The first S.S. *Roebuck* had a chequered career. In July 1911, outward bound in fog, she ran aground on the Kaines Rocks off St Brelade's Bay, but was refloated and repaired. She sank at Scapa Flow in 1915.

64. The S.S. *Stella* leaving harbour. This ill-fated ship went down off the Casquets in March 1899 with heavy loss of life.

65. The Casquets lighthouse off the west coast of Alderney.

Railways and Aviation

66.   A Western Railway train rounding the curve at St Aubin's station in 1906. Seven years later, the line was extended to La Corbière.

67.   A train at Fauvic on the Eastern line.

68.   The Eastern Railway terminus at Gorey.

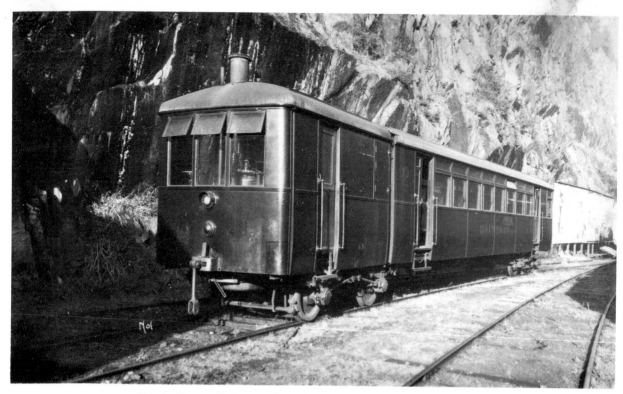

69. An Eastern Railway railcar, the *Brittany*, c.1928, in Snow Hill station.

70. First Tower station on the Western line. This railway operated for the last time in 1935, and the rolling stock was destroyed the next year by a disastrous fire. The Eastern Railway had already closed in 1929.

71. Don Bridge station in St Brelade shortly after the removal of the rails and sleepers from the permanent way.

72. The interior of the old St Aubin's terminus.

73.   The same station, now the St Brelade's Parish Hall, viewed from the cotil above, *c*.1880.

74.   La Haule station house in 1936, now the site of the Sea Sport Centre.

75.   The original West Park Pavilion, known familiarly as the Tin Hut, providing the backdrop for a passing train. The curve of West Park's Victoria Pool can be seen in the foreground.

76. An all-male gathering at Noirmont Manor on the occasion of a lunch party for the opening of Jersey Railways on 25 October 1870.

77. Jurat de Quetteville raising the Clameur de Haro against the building of the railway: an unsigned cartoon *c.*1869. The Clameur de Haro is a form of instant injunction going back to Norman times. It takes the form of an oral appeal to Rollo, Duke of Normandy (Ha! Ro!) by any man who feels himself wronged as regards his real property. As far as the railway is concerned, there were those who felt it to be an unacceptable manifestation of progress, and others who were unwilling sellers of expropriated land. The procedure for making Clameur is very specific and involves reciting the Lord's Prayer in French before witnesses. It is not to be made frivolously, under pain of heavy penalties. Jurat de Quetteville obviously felt he had good reason to risk these penalties in order to bring about the immediate cessation of operations pending the decision of the Royal Court of Jersey, which is the next step in the Clameur procedure. His raising of the Clameur delayed work on the railway but did not halt it altogether.

78.   Before the Airport was opened in 1937, the beach was used for landing and take-off. The tides ruled the time-tables and planes sometimes had to be manhandled onto the slipways to avoid an incoming tide. Here a DH Dragon is seen on very wet sand.

79.   This plane, a SARO A 19, the *Cloud of Iona*, suffered a sad accident when it crashed in the sea near the Minquiers, with the loss of all on board.

80. A SARO Windhover, with three engines high above the wing.

81. A Supermarine Seagull Flying Boat, GAAIZ, in St Helier Harbour.

82.   A row of DH 86 Express and DH Dragons lined up on the beach in 1934.

83. A DH 84 coming in to land at West Park. Note the 'spats' over the wheels.

84. A closer view showing Elizabeth Castle. Note the windsock over the rim of the pool.

85.   A Jersey Airways plane *Ouaisné Bay* at the opening of the Airport in 1937 by Mr. A. M. Coutanche, the Bailiff.

Agriculture

86. Cows being taken out to be tethered following haymaking. Note the mallet on the shoulder of the man on the left.

87. 'Le Rué Golden Princess.'

88. Another aristocrat, 'Beauchamp Sybil Reviver'.

89. This was a common sight before machine milking was introduced. To conserve pasture, cows were tethered, eliminating the need for fencing and dehorning alike.

90. This milking machine, a Gascoigne Bail, was the third to be installed in the Island, in 1933. It ran on a petrol motor until converted to electricity in 1938. The owner, on the left, was John Orange Arthur and the cowman was a Cornishman, Fred Cotton.

91. An apple-crusher, dated 1772, converted for horticulture.

92.   An apple-crusher in operation.

93.   John Dorey, a cider merchant, at Brook Farm, St John.

94. Potato planting at Bouley Bay.

95. Potato clamps in St Lawrence in the summer of 1940. Touzel John Bree, President of the Department of Agriculture, is surveying that year's crop, clamped when the approach of German armies had halted export to England. In subsequent requisitioning years he took the risk of dividing larger outlying fields with a central clamp, disguised as a boundary bank, thus saving extra supplies for civilian use.

96.   Going over the 'bridge, weighing both empty and fully-laden barrels. These are pre-1930 from their shape, the original returnable type.

97. Lorry-loads of 'earlies' at the Weighbridge about 1950. Note the more modern non-returnable barrels.

98. Conway Street at the height of the potato season.

99. Tomato picking at L'Etacq.

100. Studying the latest methods of fruit culture at the States Experimental Farm, Trinity, also known as the Howard Davis Farm. This was one of the many gifts made to the Island by T. B. Davis, a Jerseyman who made a fortune in shipping in South Africa, in memory of his son Howard who was killed in World War One. It was specifically donated in 1927 for agricultural research.

101. The most usual basic Jersey cart. Extensions could be slotted onto all four sides for vraic and other large loads.

102. This type of four-wheeled van was used for every purpose from taking potatoes to the Weighbridge to carrying Sunday School children on their annual outing. Backrests could be slotted into the sides. The hampers were the earliest containers used in the potato trade.

103. *La Grande Tchéthue*: the great plough being used in double harness.

104. An alternative ploughing technique.

105. Vraicing at Le Hocq. The collection of this valuable fertiliser was controlled in the past by law, an indication of its importance.

Island Life and Events

106.   Ceremony at Victoria College.

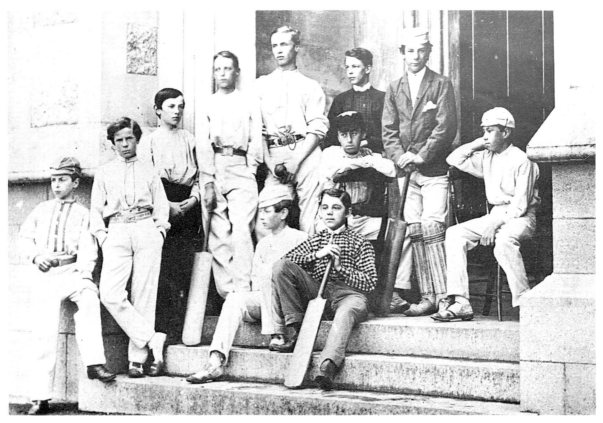

107. The Victoria College Cricket XI in 1867. At that time there were no Honours Boards, so the individuals cannot be identified, but it is known this team lost to Elizabeth College in Guernsey.

108. This shows a loan exhibition in Victoria College Great Hall in 1916, in aid of the Red Cross.

109.   An excursion to the Devil's Hole in 1903.

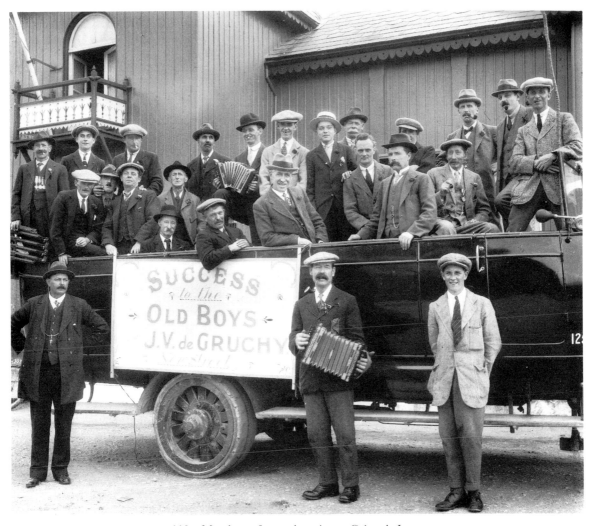

110.   Members of a coach outing at Grève de Lecq.

111.   St Aubin's Bay in the days of the bathing machine.

112.   Troops of the Royal Artillery at Elizabeth Castle.

113. Messrs. P. Mallet, P. Luce, J. Le Maistre and C. F. Le Feuvre, of the Royal Militia, taking a brief respite from their duties at Grève de Lecq.

114.   His Excellency General Gough with the Ladies' Rifle Club, *c*.1907.

115.   The First World War Prisoners of War Camp on the Blanches Banques under construction, February 1915.

116.   Jersey Militia exercises at Les Platons: 4.7 guns.

117.   The Jubilee Dinner at Victoria College in 1902. At the top table are Mr. Lester Garland, the Headmaster,
Dr. W. Duret Aubin, Dean Balleine, Mr. W. N. Venables Vernon and Canon Edward Luce.

118. A Government House garden party, *c.*1909.

119.   Another view of guests on the lawn.

120.   Guests leaving Government House, some by car.

121. St Helier's parish church bazaar and fête, September 1908.

122. The ceremony of laying the foundation stone for the *Grand Hotel*, 1890.

SILVER JUBILEE.

123.   King George V and Queen Mary's Silver Jubilee in 1935: decorations in Beresford Street.

BATH
STREET

RSEY. 1935.

124. King Street well decorated for the Silver Jubilee.

125. Queen Street vies with King Street on the same occasion.

126.   The scene in the Royal Square on 6 January 1881, the centenary of the Battle of Jersey.

127. Island choirs on the People's Park, Westmount, celebrating the coronation of King Edward VII in 1902.

128. The Vicomte R. R. Lemprière Esquire reading the Declaration of War from the plinth of the statue in the Royal Square on 4 August 1914.

129. The Battle of Flowers in 1912.

130. The Battle of Flowers at Springfield Football Ground, *c.*1930.

131. An early Battle of Flowers on Victoria Avenue.

132.   French contestants being welcomed at the harbour for the Concours Musical, *c.*1912. The Concours died out between the wars for economic reasons. At one time the landing place was Gorey Harbour, and the bands were transported to St Helier by the Eastern Railway. Attempts to revive the Concours were brought to an end by World War Two.

133. Drill practice in forming square on the Parade Ground at Fort Regent. Note the geometrical piling of the cannon balls.

134. Jersey Ladies' College, built in 1888. This early photograph was taken from the houses opposite.

135.   The College at the Headmistress's entrance. This view was probably taken on Speech Day, when until 1930 white silk dresses and long black stockings were de rigueur.

Personalities

136. Major N. V. L. Rybot in the Suez Canal area in 1914. He was a notable figure during his retirement, his contribution to the Société Jersiaise's undertakings reflecting his wide-ranging interests.

137. Mr. A. C. Godfray, M.B., L.R.C.P., L.R.C.S., in his masonic regalia. He was a founder member of the Société Jersiaise, Secretary in 1877-88 and President for three terms between 1896 and 1904.

138. A Buchan-Ireland wedding party at Le Bocage, St Brelade, in June 1872. Note the thatched roof – a fairly late survival in a house of this type.

139. The Very Rev. G. O. Balleine, M.A., Dean of Jersey from 1888 to 1906. He did much to encourage and widen the interest of the local Church and strengthen its connection with the Diocese of Winchester.

140. Mr. J. Sinel, a distinguished naturalist and archaeologist. He worked at the La Cotte cave from 1910 to 1919, and as a taxidermist created many of the exhibits of wild birds in the Museum. He was curator from 1907 until his death in 1929.

141. Mr. E. T. Nicolle, Deputy for St Helier and Vicomte. He was an active research worker and was responsible for many publications on Island history. He was also an expert horticulturist.

142. Miss Emmeline Augusta Barreau (left) was the aunt of the painter, A. H. Barreau. She presented an Art Gallery to the Société with an endowment, which included a fund for scholarships for local art students.

143. (*above left*) Mr. E. T. Touzel, a famous lifeboatman between the wars. He died in 1937. Known locally as 'Nobby' Touzel, he saved many men from drowning, and his record of life saving earned recognition from British and foreign governments. He was the recipient of a small fleet of skiffs and punts from the inhabitants of Jersey, and eked out a living hiring them. For over 40 years he was a member of the regular crew of the Jersey lifeboat, and on retiring received a pension from the Royal National Lifeboat Institution.

144. (*above right*) Judge 'Johnny' Pinel, 1864 to 1943, was Police Court Magistrate for 19 years and Judge of the Petty Debts Court from 1924 to 1943. He was also Constable of St Helier, 1910-24, and a legend in his own lifetime.

145.   Mr. Ralph Mollet, F.R. Hist. and Officier d'Academie. He was Secretary of the Société from 1946 to 1960.

146.   Jack Counter, V.C. Born in Dorset, he came to Jersey with the First Battalion of the King's Liverpool Regiment. He gained his award in France at the age of 20 for extreme bravery in carrying messages under heavy artillery fire, where others had been killed or wounded. After the war he came back to Jersey and worked in the Post Office.

147.   Two visiting archaeologists largely responsible for the successful excavations at La Cotte de St Brelade. Père Burdo worked in the cave from 1936 to 1961 and was the first to show the length of the period during which it was occupied. Professor C. B. McBurney of Cambridge University visited with his students regularly between 1961 and 1978 and showed the cave to be of international significance.

148. A group photographed in January 1925 at the French Consulate on the occasion of the unveiling of a plaque commemorating the fallen French residents of Jersey in World War One. The French General de Corn is on the right of His Excellency, Major General the Hon. Sir Francis Bingham, Lt.-Governor of Jersey. On the extreme right is Dr. Jean Labesse. On the left, against the pillar at the back, is M. Charles Dubras, President of the Comité Permanent.

General Views

149. St Catherine's Bay. In the centre is St Catherine's Tower ('White Tower').

150. La Collette: the Ladies' Bathing Place, *c*.1910.

151. La Collette: the Jersey Swimming Club's diving stage, *c*.1910. These two views are both in stark contrast to the modern idea of a swimming pool.

152.   Grève de Lecq, probably the best beach on the north coast. It has an ancient Castel de Lecq on the hill above and a Jersey type tower, built in 1780.

153.   Grève de Lecq showing a camera obscura in the small conical building, right centre.

154. Plémont. These toll-bearing staircases were the only means of access to a beautiful and popular sandy beach situated at the western end of the north coast.

155. The entrance to Valley des Vaux, at the back of St Helier; the field is tentatively earmarked for a supermarket, to replace the one-time Jersey Model Laundry.

156. L'Etacq, with Le Cappelain's *Queens Hotel* and
W. A. Vade's *Star Hotel*.

157. An archer's-eye view of Gorey Harbour and Grouville
Bay.

158. La Corbière lighthouse, with the causeway exposed. Built in 1873 on a concrete platform 9 ft. high, and the first to be made of this material in the British Isles, the tower is 35 ft. high.

159. A close-up view of the lighthouse, showing the steps and detail.

160. Hamptonne. This fine old property in St Lawrence has been acquired for development as an Agricultural Museum. The Gateway is dated 1637 and the old house inside belongs also to the 17th century.

161. Hamptonne: the courtyard on the south side.

162. Seymour Tower. This lies on an islet called L'Avarizon about 1¼ miles from La Rocque Point. It was built in 1782 in the time of General Seymour Conway, but it may be named after a much earlier tower built by Edward Seymour, Duke of Somerset, Governor *c.*1540.

163. An early view of Seafield House, Millbrook (right), before the existence of the sea wall and railway.

164.   The town of St Helier from the west, with Victoria College on the skyline, *c*.1879.

165.   The *British Hotel* in Broad Street, now Barclays Bank plc.

166.   The *Hotel Imperial*, St Saviour's Road, now the *Hotel de France*.

167.   Mont Mado. Once a genuine hill, renowned for the excellence of its stone, huge amounts were quarried from the earliest times.

168. Platte Rocque. This is near the south-east corner of the island, where the French landed in 1781 unobserved by the militiamen in the old battery. Despite an encounter with troops of the 83rd Regiment, they marched into the town without warning having been given.

169. Gorey Hill in 1896.

170. St Helier Harbour, soon after the Victoria statue was unveiled in 1890 and the garden created, and well before the nearer end of the inner basin was filled in to become a car park.

171. St Helier Harbour with deep-sea fishing boats.

172.   High Tower, St Ouen, *c.*1935. It was demolished by the Occupying Forces in 1943.